Epiphanies and Late Realizations of Love

Edited by

Claudine Nash

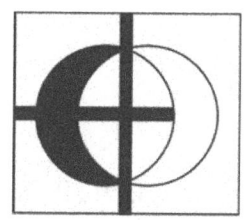

TRANSCENDENT ZERO PRESS

HOUSTON, TEXAS

Copyright © 2019, Transcendent Zero Press.

PUBLISHED BY TRANSCENDENT ZERO PRESS

www.transcendentzeropress.org

All rights reserved. No part or parts of this book may be reproduced in any format whether electronic or in print except as brief portions used in reviews, without the expressed written consent of Transcendent Zero Press, or of the respective authors.

ISBN-13: 978-1-946460-10-3
Library of Congress Control Number: 2019931549

Printed in the United States of America

Transcendent Zero Press
16429 El Camino Real Apt. #7
Houston, TX 77062

Cover painting by Vera Ikon from a concept by Dustin Pickering
Graphic design by Vera Ikon

FIRST EDITION

Epiphanies and Late Realizations of Love

Edited by

Claudine Nash

To Ella, My Beautiful Little Love
-CN

To my deceased grandmother, Faye Rollins,
without whom literature would not have come to me
-DP

Infant Joy
William Blake

I have no name
I am but two days old.—
What shall I call thee?
I happy am
Joy is my name,—
Sweet joy befall thee!

Pretty joy!
Sweet joy but two days old,
Sweet joy I call thee;
Thou dost smile.
I sing the while
Sweet joy befall thee.

"The Ying & Yang of Anna Tommy", painting by Red Focks and Ammi Romero

In Memory of Daginne Aignend

Publisher's Introduction

Regarding love and compassion, I've noted something that occurs in me and others have spoken of it as well. When I first meet someone who will eventually persuade me to love, I feel a bit of distaste for the person or a kind of self doubt. It eventually recedes and my heart sees the person differently. I am struck as if with a sudden charge of light from above after a long walk in the darkness.

Perhaps love is an epiphany. It's an opening of the eye into the nature of things. So it bewilders and shakes the consciousness of the one who perceives it. Yet it emboldens the senses and immerses them in a light that is a powerful as it is confusing.

That initial distaste, that opening resentment, is merely a way to resist it. It seduces you slowly. It's beauty overpowers you and then...you are lost to it. It owns you. You cannot let it go.

We know light is everywhere and life is dependent on it for energy and sustenance. When dark embraces the earth, we sink into quietude and rest. We cannot always jubliate and dance, right?

Perhaps the intensity of love also requires resistance— a kind of turning against in reflection, letting the passions fly everywhere without attempting to order them— that is, we close our eyes before it is time to sleep. Rest helps to store energy and conserve it. It revitalizes organisms after long engagements and efforts. Dreams take place in the moments we are not trying to order the world. God's grace flows succinctly through us in those moments we let go. The dance becomes fluid. By definition, that is the meaning of grace. As if continually preparing the lines for your part in rehearsal assists you in moving into the part on stage with no effort or trace of fear.

Love is something strange. It casts a unique light on those it touches. As a teen, I was passionately in love with a girl named Sarah. When I got older I reflected on my feelings for her and realized they were naive— I had idealized her, made her a mother because I was an infant in understanding. It was my first taste of passion so long lasting.

Age, again, teaches us grace. We've learned our first steps, we have fallen in and out of grace. We have fought, struggled, failed to understand, rejected the light and its power, given in to miserable satisfactions that led nowhere. How else are we to learn that we are the ones who are wrong?

Even at a young age, in high school, I struggled to know what love is. No one else seemed to recognize my struggle for what it was. It was tiring— the passions were intense, the battles long, the darkness deep and worrisome, the absence of God immediately assumed.

I have loved many, many times— many women, many friends, strangers, mentors, landscapes, and ideas. I have shown compassion to people who treated me poorly. I had a neighbor I learned to hate he was so abusive but I was generous to him.

Those who live in the dark may not find themselves out of it without a light.

The purpose of this anthology, given the period we live in with its divisiveness and fear, is to keep that light shining on the world. We are witnessing a lot of hypocrisy, rage, abuse of power, disrespect, thoughtlessness, racism, heated tensions, and general malcontent. The world as we know it is experiencing a drastic change— it seems to be coming suddenly, without warning, and we are not prepared for it. How do we surmount the obstacles at hand? Where do we reach our hands out to show our humanity?

Think for a moment about the nature of fear. What brings you the most worry in life? Take a look at it, think on it. Ask if it truly is the beast you make it out to be.

We can only conquer fear if we understand what it is making us afraid. Reach out to others concerning your worries. Speak to those who are open, especially if you have disagreements. Be polite, listen, and let in the dark if only to embrace a fuller understanding.

It's not always disagreement that makes for hatred. Sometimes it's petty jealousies, a desire for self-importance, a need to vent your rage, or something completely outside of the obvious causes for animosity. I can only know this because I have experienced it.

I hope the sentiments in this collection in the least bring the readers a stronger sense of self, one strong enough to transcend the Ego and its illusions. May your self-understanding improve this year and may you live peacefully in such rough times.

Dustin Pickering, Publisher

Table of Contents

Editor's Introduction by Claudine Nash / 13
A Love Poem – Susan Moorhead / 15
Cicada Moon – Susan Moorhead / 16
A Memory Evaporates – Chani Zwibel / 17
Rain-Stairs – Chani Zwibel / 18
Lovenesia – Stacey Michelle Spencer / 19
The Sun and the Grey – Kamilah Glover / 20
I Wish – Matt Borczon / 21
Dance with Me – Matt Borczon / 23
When you are Engulfed in Exhaustion – Weasel Patterson / 25
Waiting for Our Ears to Grow Dreams – Weasel Patterson / 26
Rough Lines – Sheikha A. / 27
#inbetweensonnets – Sheikha A. / 28
Dreamland – Luke Kuzmish / 29
Haiku 761,226 – Red Focks / 31
Dear Suki: #81 – Lana Bella / 32
The Melody of You – Don Beukes / 33
Gingerbread Victorian – Robert Milton Ingram / 34
Mad Love – Chuck Taylor / 36
They Called Him the Patron of Poetry – Mikayla Davis / 37
There is No Opposite to Love – Winston Plowes / 38
Virtual Love – Joan McNerney / 39
The Subliminal Room – Joan McNerney / 40
I Hate the Way You Love Me – R Bremner 42
The Vase – Lynn White / 43
Glacier – Leah Mueller / 44
This Evening is Not for Love Poems – Debasish Parashar / 46
Love in Less – Debasish Parashar / 47
The Only Boy in Ballet Class – Zack Rogow / 48
Symmetron: You and Brother Will – Zack Rogow / 50
The Pilot's Daughter – Kristin LaFollette / 51
Road Work – Kristin LaFollette / 52
Papa's Roots – Lisa Rhodes-Ryabchich / 53
We Are Beautiful Like Snowflakes – Lisa Rhodes-Ryabchich / 54
A Torrent of Words – Mary Elmahdy / 55
Five Things I Should Tell You – Lennart Lundh / 56
A Love Poem to My Teenage Self – Adam Levon Brown / 57
Imperfection – Adam Levon Brown / 59
Non-Love – Myra Ward / 61
Ode to Self-Respect – Rania M.M. Watts / 62
In This Love and Time – Marianne Szlyk / 63
Congressional Village – Marianne Szlyk / 64
After the Concert – Ethan Goffman / 65
After Copernicus Street Fair – Anton Yakovlev / 66

Afterword – Anton Yakovlev / 68
The Room Under the Temple – Annie Bien / 69
Blow Your Breath into Elephant Nostrils – Annie Bien / 70
Erophilia – Michael Estabrook / 71
Every Day of My Life – Michael Estabrook / 72
Mathew in the Fountain – Stephanie L. Harper / 73
Tremble the Sky – Robert Okaji and Stephanie Harper / 74
With Guitar in Hand – Robert Okaji / 75
When Shadows Hide – Robert Okaji / 76
Untitled – Margarita Serafimova / 77
All the Chances You Were Meant to Miss – Iris Orpi / 78
Lucas – Margaret Anderegg / 80
Song & the Bottom of the Root – Debasis Mukhopadhyay / 81
Unclaimed – Shan Spradlin / 82
Agony – Jagari Mukherjee / 83
Gleanings – Winston Derden / 84
Elements – Srividya Sivakumar / 85
Waltz – Elina Petrova / 88
Protection – Elina Petrova / 90
Ulcus Tangere - Sanjeev Sethi / 91
Dinner – Jessica Rowshandel / 92
After Twenty-Five Years – Robert Cooperman / 93
In a Universe Where – Josh Dale / 94
A Kiss from the Wind – Susan Mitchell / 95
Out of the Blue – Susan Moorhead / 96
Memory – Jessica Goody / 97
The Marriage – Kiriti Sengupta / 98
A Language Foreign – Melissa Chappell / 99
Metropolis – John Kojak / 100
Where is Love – JeanMarie Olivieri / 102
Addressing the Hall of Poets – James B. Nicola / 103
Awakening – Daginne Aignend / 104
Sitting Zazen on the Downtown Train – Claudine Nash / 105
Magnolias – Claudine Nash / 107
One – Usha Akella / 108
Sufi Poems – Usha Akella / 109
Post Script by Z. M. Wise / 108

Acknowledgements / 110
About the Authors / 111

Introduction

When the submission call for this anthology was released, we asked poets from around the world to submit poems about all aspects of love. Poems about romantic love, the process of love, love between friends or siblings, love for a child or parent, spiritual love and compassion, love for the natural world, and love for oneself were all welcome.

Certainly, the world is in no short supply of books about love, so why compile another such collection? The answer is simple. In these dark days of uncertainty and division, we wished to flood the world with love as a form of political protest. We sought to spread hope and compassion as a salve. We saw love poetry as a means of reminding us of our interconnectedness, as a tool to appreciate our different realities as well as our common humanity.

The past two years have found the world and certainly those in the United States facing new levels of conflict with frequent reports of mass shootings and acts fueled by xenophobia, anti-Semitism, racism, and homophobia spilling into our news feeds and homes. In such times it is hard not to think of leaders like Dr. Martin Luther King, Jr. who spoke so elegantly of love as a moral imperative and a powerful tool for restoring communities. In our small way, we wished to let more love seep into the cracks around us through poetry.

The words of Ari Mahler so clearly capture the sentiment of this book. A rabbi's son and the trauma nurse on duty at Allegheny General Hospital the night that Robert Bowers burst into a Pittsburgh synagogue and heinously gunned down eleven people as they prayed, Mahler chose to treat the wounded Bowers as compassionately as he would any other patient. In a post on social media Mahler later wrote, "Love as an action is more powerful than words, and love in the face of evil gives others hope. It demonstrates humanity. It reaffirms why we're all here… you, the person reading this, love is the only message I wish to instill in you. If my actions mean anything, love means everything."

We thank the contributors of this anthology for their poetry and for sharing their views and experiences with love. And we hope that by sharing them with you, our dear readers, we can spread love to you in a time when it is needed the most.

Claudine Nash

A Love Poem

Susan Moorhead

I don't write them,
those moons in June rhymes.
You're not my breath, my soul,
or my heartbeat. You don't
complete me, nor I you.
What you are is my every day,
my evening, and my night.
All these years later,
still such happiness
when I come up the street
and see your car in the driveway
and know that you are home.

Cicada Moon

Susan Moorhead

Late summer, the air soft like a tangible
thing you could hold in the cup of your hand.
No matter what the day brought, you said,
there was always that perfect moment
of rose and blues, that golden last claim
of the setting sun. A sweet chill plumed
the edges of wind stirring through the thick
darkness of trees, that old conversation
of coming and going. We were brushstrokes
on the canvas of that moment.
After you left, I listened to the whirring
rise and fall of cicadas outside
the windows, the night a milky sheet
thrown across the bed. Above the speaking
trees, the sky was a saucer on which
the night balanced, and the moon was
a small chip of porcelain above my head,
above my sleep.

A Memory Evaporates

Chani Zwibel

If I forget your street is paved with brick
will you forget the shape of my face and my name?
I drove up the hill
in the rain that wasn't cold
in the summer.
A memory evaporates
against the windshield,
and time forgets you had a name
and you lived here:
the closed road,
the empty,
weed-choked lawn,
the abandoned house.
Ten years, twenty, thirty, more…
still nothing changes.

Rain-Stairs

Chani Zwibel

I

You looked so sweet and childish
in the rain in your galoshes
with my large green and white
umbrella clasped in your hands,
your bright eyes
beneath glasses
smiled.

II

I slipped on the tiles
sliced my elbow open,
a mean mouth,
red on my shocked fingers pulled back.
You told me not to look at it;
You could fit a pencil in the gap.
We have to go to the ER.

III

We sat in the waiting room
for what seemed an eternity,
as all waiting rooms seem in all versions of time.
I remained calm, likely in shock,
reading my homework.
7 stitches sealed the cut
but the blood stained my jeans.

IV

You stayed with me
through all of it
as you would be with me
through many other hospital visits,
mishaps, accidents, funerals
you stayed.

Lovenesia

Stacey Michelle Spencer

It's like lovenesia
People tell you to let it go
And you do, not knowing
What you're letting go of
Something that moves beyond you
Is not yours to contain
Until someone puts it into words
Or you fry your mind around it
Then people contort their bodies
In search of its existence
Even those who've known it
Scrape themselves around its edge and bottom
Or maybe everyone feels it
They make a ruse of the person
Who feels it differently than they do
Takes the collective desire
And says, This is mine
He is mine
Tonight or ever after
He's a man
That's all and everything in the universe
There is to it

The Sun and the Grey

Kamilah Glover

Things aren't always as bright
as they used to be
Our colors are changing
Our leaves are withering away on our tree of love
But I hold on to the roots
There is where the foundation was built
On those sunny summer days
There is where the soil is rich
Where our love was the fertilizer
And we grew up, and tall
Together
There is where our strength is.
These days I understand your grey better
Now I know what it feels like to be used to no sun
It's a cozy place for the sorrowful
It a place of understanding
Grey gets the light and the dark and chooses neither
It just remains still.
How else can a tree grow
Without rain?
Without dirt?
Without bugs?
The grey is necessary
But for a period of time
For how also can a tree grow
Without sun?
Without seeds?
Without warmth?
I understand now the necessity of both
How my sun and your shade created a beautiful foundation in which we fell in love
And I will honor the yang in you
As long as you nurture the yin in me.
We will grow and together
For roots are far more difficult to grow apart
When they've been growing together from the start.

I wish

Matt Borczon

I could
listen
for you
really listen
to that
Leonard Cohen
song that
gentle rain
I wish
I could
find that
egg with
that horse
inside it
I wish
I could
really change
your life
with my
love
I wish
I was
one of
seven Chinese
brothers swallowing
the ocean
one of
five senses
tasting a
kiss
one of
three on
a match
of two
that makes
company
I wish
I was
an army
of one

I wish
I was
not someone
who wishes
all the
time
if wishes
were horses
beggars would
ride
if horses
were tears
then tears
would run
the plains
and fields
if beggars
could ride
I would
ride into
the eye
of a
hurricane
the heart
of darkness
the walls
or regret
the center
of the
city and
the bottom
of the
ocean to
the top
of the
mountain
never once
thinking of
pulling a gun
or running away.

Dance with me (for Dana)

Matt Borczon

between the
bus station
and the
school yard
between
hell and
high water
from here
to the
sun
dance with me
to music
and sadness
from old
age to
death from
breakfast
to lunch
we'll skip
dinner
skip the
evening news
unpaid bills
silly arguments
and the
morning alarm
clock
dance with me
until stars
fall until
wars end
until our
kids have
their own
kids until
all the
kids have
grown until
the world
ends not
with a

bang but
a whimper
soft and
beautiful
like the
way the
ocean swallows
the moon

when you are engulfed in exhaustion

weasel patterson

we are sleeping together
your head soft against my shoulder
breath warming my ear
while the air conditioner
turns our room into a freezer

i count the dust on the ceiling
trying to figure when it was born
and how long til it finally is ready to pass

your mouth whispers something
but i couldn't hear it
it's funny how often that happens
even when you're awake
i can't hear you

you have said i am welcome
to walk inside
yet i can't make a home
inside your bones

embers of your flesh
have grown cold
carrying fragments
we can't regain

you tell me you love me
and i still don't know how
to tell you that my skull
is consumed
by your emptiness

waiting for our ears to grow dreams

weasel patterson

the moon is a half-shell
drifting above us

i followed her for you
not understanding
that some prayers
can only be answered
by looking inward

i bound my ears
filled caverns of my heart
to stop her stars
from leading me astray

i wanted to get lost
in the currents
of your pulse

my hands grip your body
close to mine
forgetting that love
isn't just a wet dream

that magic, doesn't burst into life
without you

Rough Lines

Sheikha A.

Blooms on a hill, and I ask: do you
really want to suffer a life of

my tyranny - a numen moon like
a jawing apocalypse. You smell

flowers on mud because you believe
we are distinguished destinies on remedial

marrow; our blood is the task of different
oceans - jellyfish trapped in willow nets.

Your eyes are black deserts of non-
conforming winds. Milky sands on

the water's edge. How does one learn
to love a box not opened to giving;

I am trying to build a rhythm in fixed
patterns. Ghost the light, you say, we will

build a kayak for running when our feet
turn to nail-less toes. So much planned.

I'm sitting on my bed watching paths break
as gifted visions. Don't tell me I will lose

in love. One river flows in my body
right now. It tastes of heaven's broken gate.

#inbetweensonnets

Sheikha A.

but balanced in the space between
unready and unopened
- Night School by Mary McCarthy

Much of me has receded. Beauty of
sparkling grapes: a void-full bulb of
fire-moulded eyes. This is how I bring
myself to you: packing in numbers,
countless counting, repetitively fickle,
in a state of sweltering, spread on
the gridle of a sea-moon. Don't come
like the valour idealising flesh, quotes
about open concepts of love. You will
encounter a reptilian stare pretending to
read the soul unattached from your body,
and convert to a near-true description
of me, the kind that causes distress to
lulled hurricanes. If you should think
of holistic readings based on a picture
of my face, be sure to counsel from
an edifice of a water-mind. The hours in
my day cost a wearying varnish. Chips of
old paint fall like over-clung hail. If my eyes
were a prison of winters that snowed,
you would be the water that froze me
into a crescent shaped arrow.

dreamland

Luke Kuzmish

maybe we can cuddle in dream land

maybe
just maybe
the rattling head boards
against the flop house walls
will sound
like my beating heart
pressed to your ear

in dream land
you'll shiver
from love
vulgar love
and
an unvulgar romance
instead of the wind
cutting through
your comforter

where your lips
will be wet
with no alcohol
on your breath

where the whispers
are not of radiators
groaning to start
but of my incantations
to bring your spirit
back
from splintered pieces

maybe in dream land
your heart
made useful
rather
than made busy

maybe in dream land
distance

is a lesson
learned
without
pain

'un retrato de familia", painting by Red Focks and Ammi Romero

HAIKU 761,226

Red Focks

Gonna build a wall.
I'll dig a hole when I'm sad
and give you kisses.

DEAR SUKI: #82

Lana Bella

Dear Suki: Aubade, June, 1976,
You were late to this thing called
giving-up, folding over like a tide.
Against the blind where the night-
stand light illumed yellow, I stood
ordinary in the irises of your eyes,
hands diametrically at odds reach-
ing the abstract of you. The world
I knew was dark, perhaps you had
shifted under with the lit cigarette
of my body, in this way I was ever
wending, a cursive starling for you.
But you broke black becoming one
with time like a bad migraine, soft
mouth tossed back what the nights
hungered, body bled out into some-
one else's mouth, bearing my name.

The Melody of You

Don Beukes

The first notes I heard from you were echoes of your gentle heartbeat resonating through my whole being igniting my dormant essence with your sparks of life-giving cherry kisses sweetening my bitter memories of failed romances missed chances of love ever after – Your voice soothing my brittle heart lowering my forced guard of imprisoned feelings liberated from daily trappings of hate and self-doubt even daily aimless cadaver walks passing familiar shared places ignoring friendly familiar sympathetic faces.

I am now floating on your symphony uplifting – Your musicality saving my love sick fatality, your intricate intoxicating nuances taking me to new unknown emotive places never before experienced until you floated into my tone-deaf life like a sweet melody demanding my attention – Your inner rhythmic beat mesmerizing calming reassuring, swirling my deepest emotions to places I could only dare dream of –

Your laugh a gentle waterfall breaking over smooth polished pebbles creating a lasting memory of our new shared melody as I willingly submit to the melody of you the essence of you the radiance of you the symphony of you the aroma of you the aura of you, the whole of you –
Our love anew...

Gingerbread Victorian

Robert Milton Ingram

I drove by the old house today—
that magnificent Gingerbread Victorian
just two blocks from Ivy Green,
where Helen Keller rediscovered
the gift of language and life
and where our life together
fell apart.

For nearly a century and a half
the bay window up front
must have witnessed countless battles
against nature, nations, neighbors,
and namesakes.

The house sits empty now that
the latest tenants have moved out.
No sounds of laughter echo off the plaster walls;
no fires crackle in the decorative fireplaces;
no couples share romantic dinners
under the antique chandelier;
no children slide in their stocking feet across the
wooden floors.

But that will all end soon.
Another young family will surely discover
the charms of this place,
and all will be as it should be
once again.

I could not resist the temptation
to walk up onto that sturdy porch
whose brick columns have welcomed many
a visitor.

I sat on the floor beneath the hooks
where the swing once hung.
I looked up to the corner
where the bird nest
once sat.

Every spring a pair of young doves
would come and make their nest
in that corner. And when the babies
had learned to fly, another couple,
like clockwork, would show up
within two days, and lay its eggs.
Every year, I would swear
it was the same two
pairs of doves.

The summer that I painted the porch
I took great care not to touch the nest—
even though it was empty at the time.
I thought it would be a sacrilege
to disturb it. It's gone now.
The last tenants must have
swept it away.

Another spring is fast approaching,
and I wonder if the doves
will ever return to that
grand old house.

Mad Love

Chuck Taylor

to say a word for our common tabby cat,
to say a word for Oliver, senile now,
my friends say, inside always now too,
after the latest flap with a pack of dogs
chasing him to a hiding place it took
three days for him to come out of,
old gimpy arthritic cat who we found
in the garage after we bought the house,
cat who we named Spook at first because
you rarely saw the ninja warrior streaking
from the food dish we set under the
ping-pong table, but now an old purrer
of laps and sleeping on your head in bed,
Oliver, who has chosen me, out of some
cat irrational need, to love best,
though I never feed, though I have a
backyard dog I take for country walks
and have never liked cats, Oliver, lumbering
across the floor, those large doe eyes
looking up in mad love, begging an ear rub,
a neck scratch, Oliver, Oliver, you could love
my good mate, the one who bathes you
the one who pulls off your fleas
and trims your nails--but no, it's me
and only me, could it be my fabulous
finger technique?--come on, give in,
the mute glowing cat orbs say,
let me on your lap, take this broken
love and learn to tolerate
so you learn to love--
for you are broken too, eh?
and mad like me for love

They Called Him the Patron of Poetry

Mikayla Davis

and I used to sit behind the fallen
tree as I listened to him read
out loud to the group around him,
campfire swallowed by his hair,
his face an ember in the black
of midnight swamp.

His voice began as a tingle
against the skin, just enough to raise
hairs on my arm like the perking
of ears. I'd tilt my head
in an effort to get closer,
like that urge to curl into
a comforter in the winter,
arms around my waist.

The words rose, like air dancing
from the hot asphalt of the hotel
parking lot, and my breath
twirled with them like tangled sighs
until dizzy at just a phrase. I forgot
how my lungs worked, a hand
pressed against my chest.

And then he would stop, go quiet,
and I'd burst, my eyes stinging
as I wiped away the tears
I didn't know had begun to fall.
I'd laugh, throaty and wet,
confused about why my heart
was flickering so fast. I'd look around,
trying to see if anyone
was as fueled as me.

There Is No Opposite To Love
After Freedom of Love by Andre Breton

Winston Plowes

My Husband with the skin of plastic rain
With the forgetfulness of cold sun
With the neck of a snake in the claws of a dog
With the lips of unspoiled earth,
With the voice of stroked jet and pumice
My Husband with the voice of a child that closes
and opens its mind
My Husband with the eyebrows of a punch,
With lashes of the centre of an eagle's sky
My Husband with the chin of screams
with legs like landslides with minnows' tails above the debris
My husband with ankles of tree stumps
My Husband with knees of violin wood and conkers
With legs of the loneliness of chaff in the field
My husband with arms of guttered candles
With the stillness of random joy
My Husband with lowercase hands
With hands of square locks
My husband with a waist of pearled wheat
My husband with a stomach of the hills of silver
Of a divorce in the very chair of trickles
My husband with a chest of emerald gossip
My husband with the chest of a dog coming home
With a chest of slow gold
With a chest of the dark
My husband with shoulders of a liner
With shoulders of cannonball steel
My husband with the desire of sand and sugar
My husband with the desire of winter
With the abstinence of a weed
My husband with the abstinence of matte black paint

Virtual Love

Joan McNerney

A
long
slim
poem
full of hyperbole
& alliteration drifted
into the wrong e-mail box.

There she met an erudite
rich text format file.
They became attached.

Her fleeting metaphors
lifted his technical jargon.
They were a word couple
spinning through cyber space
giddy with inappropriate syllables.

The Subliminal Room

Joan McNerney

That weepy October
marigolds were so full.
I made an omelet with
them. Do you remember?

All November, leaves
mixed with rain, making
streets slippery. We
listened mostly to Chopin.
Leaves droop in September
too ripe and heavy for
trees. I was careful
not to slip, dreading
when leaves would grow
dry and crumble.
Some live all winter
through the next spring.
Chased by winds, they
huddle in corners,
reminding me of mice.

I confessed to you
how I loved Russian
poets and waited for
a silent revolution,
revealing my childhood
possessed by rosaries
and nuns chanting Ave,
Ave, Ave Maria. "Your
navel exudes the warmth
of 10,000 suns," you said.

We still live in this
subliminal room.
Jonah did not want to
leave the whale's stomach.
We continue trying to
decipher Chopin. Your
eyes are two bunches of
morning glories. Sometimes
the sky is so violet.

Will we ever live by the sea, Michael, and eat carrots? I do not want my sight to fail. Hurry, the dew is drying on the flowers.

I hate the way you love me

R. Bremner

I hate the way you love me
like a cat playing with a mouse
letting me go free for an instant
than slamming your paw on my tail
so I have nowhere to go
but back to you.

"never ever be apart", painting by Marcel Herms

The Vase

Lynn White

The kitchen looked tired and worn
like my mother did,
the last time I saw her there.
I felt no nostalgia for it.
It was not my childhood kitchen.
It held no special memories,
I thought.
And then,
I saw the vase on the counter top.
My friend found it on the Kings Road.
Bought it and brought it home.
I'd asked her to buy me something,
a souvenir of swinging London.
She bought the vase.
I never much liked it.
Dark and bulbous,
it spent most of its time at my mother's,
though she didn't like it much either.
Then time stole it away,
took it from my memory,
erased it.
And now,
here it is again, sharp as ever
bringing the past home
as it stands empty
on the counter top.
It seems that her death
invested in it a poignancy
that it had not known before.

I took it home with me.

Glacier

Leah Mueller

I know we've arrived home
by the pine scent, and you
almost smile as we climb
from the car, say

"it smells so good
here." I agree, notice
how thin your face looks now,
and how your jeans used to be
much fuller. We've had

a severe year, without pause
in the trenches, and I can feel
the strain in your teeth and shoulders:
those shoulders your parents
taught to hide from confrontation.

You need three days
to relax, after countless doses
of forest medicine, administered
one dropper at a time.

At the waterfall,
I have trouble parking the car
and it reminds you of
your other problems, all

the angles you can never reach. Still,
you steer in reverse, into a parking
spot, and we walk uphill
until the road swallows us whole.

We return to our sanctuary.

The previous day, we
climbed much higher, to Artist Point,
followed the switchbacks
and watched two young boys
run downhill through boulders
as if falling was impossible.

We know stumbling
is inevitable, and we walk
gently through rubble, gaze
at blue-plated lakes, shiver
as fall arrives. The glacier recedes,
but the chill moves in harder than ever.

Later, we drink wine, watch
a sixteen year-old movie:
two bodies curled together on a plaid couch
beside the Nooksack. The years
rage by like angry water, and we
fail to pay attention. We must
be taught to remember.

This Evening Is Not for Love Poems

Debasish Parashar

This evening is not for love poems
We can just sit quiet and indifferent
You know what I mean?
You know I know
It is fine even if you don't
I still remember that sweet December
You sitting by my side
Life was so beautiful
I still remember you holding a green umbrella against a sophist sky
grey with tales
And your eyes rainy with words
It did rain that evening
It really rained
This evening is not for love poems
This evening is not for love poems
This evening is political
This red river of blood that separates us and unites You and Me is a political triumph
This indifference is strategic
A Panopticon of hope
Still imprisons me like the bronze statue from Harappa buried for ages
Just to be alive
This evening
Let us rather dream
Like they do in love
Let us be rebels for a cause
Like they do in love
Let us doubt, disagree and deny
Like they do in love
Conflict is a hungry chameleon dancing wild in a puritan carnival
And a carnival is true
This evening is not for sweet love poems
This evening is too many and too much

Love in Less

Debasish Parashar

I had never believed
love
could be expressed
in a haiku
or a short poem

precise
like a wink

social
like senses

multiple
like a word

Then I loved
and
thank god
I realized
no need
for love
to be a gaze
if profound

like a glimpse.

The Only Boy in Ballet Class

Zack Rogow

I know what you're thinking
but it's not exactly about that.

It's about galaxies
of Austrian crystal dimming
as I shifted in my scratchy velvet seat.
The curtain was hiked up
and suddenly the pancaked dancers,
the costumes, and cut-out castles
beamed more real than daylight.

"Look how the cavalier partners her," my mother nudged
during the pas de deux.
The male launched the prima ballerina, letting her
fly. "Look how masculine he is,"
my mother admired.

I knew she was placing in my hands a message
about sex, about how to love a woman.

But when does the cavalier get to shine? I wondered.

Only when he soloed, it turned out.
Then he
                              leaped into the music.
              Suspended.
Stretching time.

And my mother's message about the pas de deux
didn't mention where
a woman's desire was hiding,
like a lost continent.

So I began my life as a lover
with an obstructed view. Then

I dated a divorcée
who didn't believe
a woman's pleasure
just tags along after.

I started to carry the guilt
of all men for that deliberate ignorance,
while she taught me to play her cavalier.

I learned that dance well,
but still I had to find the man
behind the ballerina,
the one who only leaped
when the stage was empty.

Symmetron: You and Brother Will

Zack Rogow

                                 Shakespeare never got to see
    a Monet. Never gazed into liquid mirrors
                          of the Seine.
               Yet he knew how to describe
a sateen shadow.
                   He could speak beauty
                as well as anyone
                                  who has a special ear
for the cool
of a stream or the curves
                      of a song.

              Someone could write a song
                   about the curves
of your cool
        pomegranate lipstick, how a tongue awakens your ear.
  Sometimes it feels to this particular anyone
         as if your beauty
is part shadow,
        part the highest prime number. I need to describe
  you, how you make me crazy and sane
                            as I look into your eye mirrors
  that Shakespeare was never lucky enough to see.

The Pilot's Daughter

Kristin LaFollette

The thing you wanted to do most—

Wings like paper maps folded

time and time
again,

a red dot for each person who
knew you, for each person
who knew about the ground

that fall,

no snow decaying into the dirt,
creating a frozen layer of skin—

The ground, still wet with summer,
soft under your body, your blood
still
       warm

like an animal burrowed deep
in a hole,   heart pumping blood
into the earth, attached,
breathing,

but just barely,
as if asleep.

On a cold day in the back of a truck,
I watched a runway—

A young boy (your son), in jeans and a red jacket,

a young woman (me,
                     your daughter),

in a black coat, eyes to the sky.

Road Work

Kristin LaFollette

The road is dark
as we drive, two
hours from home

A yellow balloon in
the backseat, the radio
station cutting in and out

You've grown into a
strong young man—
I can hear your heart
beating as you sit in

the seat next to me,
the sound like a
Midwestern snowstorm—
Such a hot night,
but I can smell
the mineral smell of
ice, see your 17 year

brown skin,

Imagine a smaller
version of your hand
outreached, fingers
splayed, stretching like
a web across a

windowpane.

Papa's Roots

Lisa Rhodes-Ryabchich

for my father

Kindness loomed above all his efforts.
He found a family home & made it blossom,

by salvaging a one-hundred-year-old barn
with three stories, attached to

a dilapidated shed & tarnished metal
water pump pumped fresh well water,

tasting natural like brook water, falling
over the soft cilia-like moss breathing,

with minerals, that nourished papa's roots
allowing them to grow & mature.

Papa's plans were bubbling
with new inventions in renovations—

a ghost-inhabited barn unkempt
& impoverished with an acre.

Sour grapes grew on a vine—
Papa easily turned them into wine.

A large barn door slid open
with a hard thrust,

especially when it rained.
This period lasted like fermenting wine,

chilling in the cellar
underneath the stained-glass windows,

hanging from a black frame,
that opened & closed with a tiny lever.

We Are Beautiful Like Snowflakes

Lisa Rhodes-Ryabchich

What a beautiful pink cloud, Floating by, high up in
The sky. Looks like Snow, for tomorrow… Let it snow
Let it snow… so we can fly high, free, in the Blue
Glorious sky, like a snowflake, so beautiful
Crystalline, a living Spirit, spreading vibrant
Energetic pulses, across the Universe
Like syncopated drops, of *Light bursts*—miracle
Powder, awakening the World, to a wondrous
Magical, new moment— another Glorious
World, all the way to a new dimension, of mother-
Human Spirit— a path across the skyway, ripples
Like a human heartbeat, keeping you *Alive*, with
The hands, of a great *God,* invisibly connected
To everything, and everyone, like the love, that gives
Birth, when a baby takes, her first Voice lesson, in
The Delivery Room and her face wants an arm, to
Burrow into, and the Words, "I'm so happy to
See you," coming through her mother's Lips, smiling with
Ecstasy, saying: You are the first, and Lastborn—
The legacy of Us— the seed that will flourish
Beyond the walls, that don't Need to be here, and you
Will sour into flight, like a *New*star— a rare being—
An incredible Gift, you are every second, every day, flows
The rest, of your God-given, beautiful natural life!

A Torrent Of Words

Mary Elmahdy

A torrent of words
 Sent in haste
 Spellchecker distortions
And all.

The wait for reply
 As slow as the
 Erosion of bedrock
"It's not you. . . "
 And then, the deluge.

Five Things I Should Tell You

Lennart Lundh

One
I know where flowers go when the holy water
of being loved evaporates, the firmament
is sucked back in time to a moment before
Creation, and all the processes sustaining
immortality end in silent asphyxia.
The keyed Pandora's Boxes of our hearts'
histories hold them, keeping us safe
as long as we're not foolish.

Two
If I give you my spare change,
the last penny above the pocket lint,
or the grateful shape of my soul
as it rises steam-like one fine day,
would you feel more wanted or less?
Take all the time you want to decide.

Three
When I knew my body was meant for you
eternally instead of the time being,
instead of until Death does us,
then I began to crave reincarnation.

Four
If you knew the burn in my memory
of your lipstick, the permanence
of your lashes beneath my kiss,
you would understand the whole
of Eternity and Grace at once.

Five
I need you to know
the longest lonely is done
with each good morning.

A Love Poem to my Teenage Self

Adam Levon Brown

Pain and sorrow painted
him with brush strokes of neglect
and heartbreak;

if only for one midnight-drunk
second,

I want to show him
how the moon has robbed him
of star-lit kisses,

The way my heart
is an unpinned grenade
when I think of him

Sending a catapulted
sigh into Heaven's lungs

If two feet can walk
a mile,

Just imagine how far
the imagination
can lunge forward
with empathy
in its moon-supple
hands

Ready to hold
and untie the variety
of nooses he harbors daily

The many nooses
he stores in his closet
and puts around his neck

I want to tell him that fragility
is not a sign of weakness,
but a sign of good will

And then show
him how far compassion
can inch its way
to the breakers
of joy

In this ocean
we call life

Imperfection

Adam Levon Brown

A body left unscathed is like a book unread
no tatters, and no growth to behold

I have parallel scars on my hips
from my teenage years from wearing
tight low riding jeans to fit in with
the wannabe gangstas.

I have scars on my hands from razor
blades and cigarette burns when those "Friends"
went away

I have a surgery scar on the top of my right index
finger, from when I got in a fight with my older brother
in the swimming pool at my old apartment in 2004

I later swam with the cast on when I was on a trip
to San Diego.

I have freckles all over my shoulders from the massive
scabs developed during the time in San Diego, because
I decided not to use Sunscreen

I have a jagged scar on my right thigh
from when I was 10 because I played
with knives a lot. The bandage I made
was of paper towels and neosporin

I went without brushing my teeth for years
and I'm soon to get denchers,
from too much soda pop while celebrating
life

I now have gray hairs streaming along my beard
and head where there were none just a year ago.

I have the name of my first love scarred on my arm
in a vain attempt to self-tattoo when I thought things would last forever

I have blackheads, and a strange lump on the left side
of my head which I've had for 6 years and haven't given much thought.

I am balding in areas, stretched back in time where I used to make fun of my dad and grandpa for having bald spots

I have compassion lines on my forehead, and empathy
bags under my eyes from sleepless nights, worrying
about those worse off than I.

My fingernails are usually untrimmed, my face, not shaven,
my clothes, not spotless, and my smile at myself in the mirror, is still rarely broken.

I love myself.

Non-Love

Myra Ward

A bruised girl presented with
candles glimmering to music,
wine glasses set for two,
hearing "this night is for you",
giggles and asks "is this a movie ?"

To her, love is getting to hold
his pool stick while he goes to smoke.

Melodic minutes, tender times
gifted by white knights,
a bruised girl cannot understand.

She isn't dumb.
She is rigidly numb.
Eons may pass before she
overcomes Non-Love.

Ode to Self-Respect

Rania M.M. Watts

I alone can stand on the foothills
of the snow-capped Himalayas,
where Yeti resides in peace.

I can dive
to the depths of the ocean's floor,
where a giant squid & sperm whale may spar,
exorcise all the gothic demons who
haunt me in the pitch shadows.

I can see whose spirit
is brought back from the land of the dead
with the crow perched on my window sill,
watch as a planet's oceans transform to blood
with all the poached shark fins.

I alone can embrace
the fortification of the rays
in spite of the sphere's rejection.

I observe
this world as it aches...
when most of humanity lies idle.

I will never
look through another's eyes
to seek approval.

I am me
for once in my life!

In This Love and Time

Marianne Szlyk

He is asleep down the hall,
expecting you there,
expecting you
to leave when he does,
when empty buses slosh
down emptier streets,
when sleep finally comes.

You look up from your book
on the greasy table.
The heavy door slams.
Feet pound upstairs.
The last punk club
in Kenmore Square
has now closed.

You hope no one asks you
what you're reading.
The man across the hall
almost speaks. Instead
he nods.

You're free
to keep reading Keats or
to grab your purse, hail a cab,
and finish reading
alone in bed.
You're also free
to return to the room
where you will not sleep,

where you'll sit in the armchair,
and watch the lights
of late-night drivers
wash through his room
until dreams of love
and freedom finally come.

Congressional Village

Marianne Szlyk

One year we lived in an apartment
with a balcony that I sat on
only once. My husband and I
preferred to sprawl
inside, out of the glare.
From there we could see
our stained-glass pane
that we had hung outside.
Its red and blue birds
were pausing
on their way south.
Fleeing a winter
that would never come,
they kept us company

until we,
like migrating birds,
moved on.

After the Concert

Ethan Goffman

Fireflies light up and vanish, strewing patterns
more gorgeous than our neighbor's Christmas lights display.
She is lighting up the night to show off;
they are lighting up the night
to breed
to survive as a species.

A bullfrog chorus thrums
in great bass patterns
through the sticky night air
pumping out music
thrumping out "we must endure"!

E.O. Wilson would be proud
of the thronging life
on display.
Our planet is not dead yet.

In the distance
a scattering of lanterns through the thick trees
lights up the curving path
in a lovely dance with nature
centering a picture
the art of human symmetry and the primal darkness
completing each other.

A cosmic harmony
behind the great hall's curving stone pillars
after the concert.

The electronic dazzle
of the music
lingers
in the sinews of our being.
We had sought it out, thrilled to it.

Yet this little scene,
this remnant of nature's grace
that we chanced upon
sneaking away from the crowd
completes the night.

After Copernicus Street Fair

Anton Yakovlev

In love for the very first time
at the age of twelve,
I stroll with Sergey and Ilya
past a Crazy Bus, a sci-fi Ferris Wheel.
Seagulls circle a garbage heap from
a quickly dismantling circus.

No one knows my secret.

No one will guess
why I got a 5% on that reading quiz
the day my beloved came to school
in an Audi with a broken headlight,
a twisted hood
and a broken heart.

The fireworks begin.

Some pigeons take flight.
We throw garbage to imitate them.
Driven back home in some backseat,
I pray for the Audi to bend its bumper
back into a smile
and hope, most of all, that she wasn't scared.

Years pass.

Letters from my beloved,
now six time zones away,
get lost on a shelf with video games,
unanswered until it is much too late
and I can no longer find her
in any of the world's yellow pages.

The graying birds on my wallpaper
followed her mood every day—
soaring, worrying, falling,
missing each other.

But now the birds are simply frozen in flight.

In fact, they're not even birds,
just wallpaper.

Afterword

Anton Yakovlev

Coke Zero was easy to drink, and memorial benches
were always there for existentialism.
Every night he spoke to her in French,
climbed rocks and painted Russian eggs. He teased
her with inside jokes and some old scars,
but gently. Both enjoyed a warm Skype spat.
Their friendship was two comfortable cars
in adjacent lanes. She always wore her hat
and he his reticent black coat. Sour spies,
serial killers, vendors, even circus bears
high-fived them all the time, but never pried
because, well, frankly, who cares.

And that was largely fine with him. After all,
no soldiers ever blew up on the nearby shore.
His land line never woke him up with death calls
from relatives. Whenever he was bored
he could log in and see if she was online.
She usually was. Another joke to tell,
another anecdote from their separate lives
to make him sit up straight. What the hell,
he wasn't Richard Cory—not now, not ever.
He'd always have too many iTunes tracks
to try, too many free solos to savor
and migratory birds to welcome back.

The Room Under the Temple

Annie Bien

Afternoon seeps through tree limbs in the temple
courtyard, an autumn glow bathes the monk's room
where you sit, your eyes magnified by thick-rimmed glasses.
Absorbed with reading, your legs wrapped
under a wool blanket, a navy sweater warms
your angular frame.

On the table next to your bed, your prayers rest,
stacked in long sheaves, well-fingered, dormant
until evening.

You look up, eyes creasing in delight. Inside me,
tucked petals unfurl, wings of energy fly.
You invite me to sit. I settle on the corner
of your bed next to the bucket holding a sponge,
a cloth, and cleanser. You say, *I've had a cough.*
With yellow. But my lungs are better now.
I want you to last forever. Our temporariness floats.

I place into your hands the translation I made,
what you asked me to do. It's been scrubbed, placed
through a sieve to filter out the muddier phrases,
and a voice for the healing Medicine Buddha
emerged. You turn the pages reading, your eyes moisten
with tears. My breath catches. You blow your nose.

Ever my teacher, you test me: on definitions, word choice,
on meaning. You hear between breaths and take my hand.
Your attendant opens a glass case, removing a golden
scarf, a *kata*. From his hand to yours, you turn to me,
Thank you. The kata engulfs me.
Then you bow your head into my hands.

I should be bowing to you, but your head stays.
My fingers imprint the shape of your head, your cropped
grey hair, your smooth crown inside me. I place my head
close to yours and you whisper: Come back tomorrow.

Blow your breath into elephant nostrils

Annie Bien

the curl of a curious trunk
ties your longing
to the low rumble deep in the earth,

this shared breath releases
deep unsought thoughts
knitting together the pulse of all sentient beings
between each other's breaths.

You caress my arm
with your fingered trunk.

This orb rotates, spinning breaths
to other galaxies,
where stars glisten
with pulsed rhythm
to the low rumble deep
within all dream times

and every night
when I close my eyes, I bid
you sweet dreams, *lala salama,*
little ones who rescue us
from our mind made hardships.

Lala salama

Erophilia
Love of Romance

Michael Estabrook

Silence
When she would fall asleep
her pretty head upon my shoulder
I'd stay still as a stuffed otter
listening to the silence
all around me.

First Date
Asking her
to go steady with me
on our very first date 50 years ago
is the greatest thing
I've ever done in my life.

Pure Beauty
Looking up at me holding
my hand tightly telling me "Yes
I'll go steady with you
be your girl
if you still want me."

Time Travel
To go back in time
fall in love all over again:
her hair, her walk, her kiss,
her scent, her smile –
what could be better than that?

Every Day of My Life

Michael Estabrook

All those years ago, back in college,
her hair so long and lustrous,
her skirts so skimpy and short.

She's in New York City
waiting with some girl friends,
talking to some boys outside a theatre,

when one of them says,
barely able to speak in her presence,
as he stared (like he'd just seen an angel),

at her long, shiny brunette hair
flowing down around
her shoulders and back, "I can't believe
I'm standing here talking to you."
I've known exactly how he felt
every day of my life.

Matthew in the Fountain
August 1999, age 14 months

Stephanie L. Harper

In the spray's scattering
of afternoon rays
      you pass before the sun
a toddling pointed-toe satellite
eclipsing all
but its faint red ghost

Summer haloes you in sun-white down
mottling the concrete's cool glisten
like a memory from the womb

Watching the world swim into focus
in your smart brown eyes
      your round cheeks
flushing with the kisses of angels
showering from the sky   I realize
in a shutter's split-second
        I've traversed eternity

My child   you burst open my heart like the sun
bursts infinitely open each fountain drop

Tremble the Sky

Robert Okaji and Stephanie L. Harper

When you say forward, I hear roots
shouldering through the earth's unjust

clutches, reclaiming their naked skin's
luminous truth in the depths

of sustenance. When you say yes,
the grasses shiver and swallow your

salty acquiescence, no note slipping
away unsaid. I want new words
to speak this savor that rouses me
from my sacrum of shadows; I want

to tremble the sky with the triumph
of wren-song, and release the evening

sun's kiss from oblique captivity
with my answer to your whispers

at my ear and neck. When you say we,
your voice is the rain buttressing a bed

of intertwining stalks rising in taut
clasps, and uncurling their tendrils

into every cloud-break, to fill
with light until their petals burst

and the day blossoms anew,
its fragments gathered, held

in their lingering scents, each
drop glistening, whole, again.

With Guitar in Hand

Robert Okaji

With guitar in hand I observe the green beetles bumbling about,
the way they careen and crash and flail aimlessly, but to a purpose.

Sometimes I attempt one note, only to strike another, or plucking
three strings simultaneously, focus on the discordant one,

which is, of course, me. How do we live the right song?
Which casual arrangement sends us plummeting to the grass,

hearts racing? I recall thinking "this cannot be," yet could not,
would not, turn away. I bang out a minor seventh, sing a few

words, adjust my arthritic grip. Yesterday I couldn't form
the chord shapes I desired. Today the hands float along the

fretboard, unimpeded. I wish you were here. I wish
I could shift time signatures with neurotransmissions,

that we were somewhere else, out of the way, alone
but for birds chirping in the branches by the window.

I wish my flawed tunes could merge with moonlight
and compose pearlescent pieces, and that you would

sing them to me from the threshold of our shared lives. I want
everything, but cherish what we can hold in these wondrous

times. I think of your hair and eyes, how my heart
flutters to the floor and refuses to rise until your smile

unwraps the day's gift to me, defying Newton's third law,
offering unheard chords. I listen to your silences, as I do

your words, knowing the value of each. Gazing at your
photo, I speak your name, set down the guitar. Make music.

When Shadows Hide

Robert Okaji

I breathe when you breathe,
and watching me,
you capture each lost molecule.

This book blinks whenever you turn the page.
I see you between the words, between the white threads.
You are the adored chapter, the one I read in bed before
sleep, and after I wake, before the first wren announces
dawn, then in the afternoon's highest point, when shadows hide,
and later, as they emerge to stroke your bare shoulder.

What's on the other side, you ask. What do you hear?

Your breath, I say. Your name.

Untitled

Margarita Serafimova

I was in love,
and the body was everything,
and the body did not matter.

"We touch like cripples", painting by Marcel Herms

All the Chances You Were Meant to Miss

Iris Orpi

And in the end
you won't really be able to tell
if you really loved them
or only thought you did,
but sincerely.
After enough distance,
the heart becomes
an unreliable source
of information about the past.
Certainty is some
graffiti on the wall
you glimpsed at
sitting on a moving train;
the mind takes
creative liberties through time.
You were sure you saw it,
but what did it look like?
What did it say
and was it speaking to you, or
did you just unintentionally
intercept someone else's message,
love someone else's love?
How you used to get
so bent out of shape
by the mere mention of a name.
How bleak the nights were,
how everything tasted
like the color gray.
How freedom was such
a desperately terrible thing,
and how you got so crushed
by the weight of
each brand new day.
In the end you're not really sure
that any of them
were what you wanted,
or if you just wanted
to want something,
to give your loneliness
something to do,
and squeeze yourself

into the airtight little space
of not getting, or
of getting but not keeping
and see how much
you can get yourself to bleed.
You think maybe you wish
to hop back on the train,
go back in time
and tell your brokenhearted
younger self that in the future
she would find her way,
so stop hurting so much.
But really, you won't remember
enough of the old pain
to do all that.
It's not the same window.
You have seen
and wanted new things.
You cannot cry the old tears
nor invoke the old aches
to say it
the way she needs to hear it
so that she might believe you.
All there is to show
is a handful of verses
that occasionally shock you
with their intensity
and an eloquence
you admit you cannot trust,
and a heart that is strong
that sometimes fools you into
thinking it's always been strong.

Lucas
(for Mary, his mother)

Margaret Anderegg

God bless this day I thought would never come!
Your sleeping, weightless body
is placed within my arms, at last.
Now your eyes open to take us in.

Our blue eyes meet yours,
 intensely dark.
What distant mysteries they tell,
 but do not find us strange.
You smile.
Your slender almond fingers cling to mine.
My husband, Malcolm,
 strokes your silken arms.

You speak,
 your baby babbling softly echoing
 strains of a Korean lullaby.

We will call you Lucas,
 the one small thing that we can do for her
 from whose suffering comes our greatest joy --
 a child of our own.
Oh, child of my own,
Welcome Home!

Song & the bottom of the root

Debasis Mukhopadhyay

Go, I am to reclaim you as a song that misfits the memorabilia. A song that rustles through from branch to branch pecking, over and over, at all the blossoms cramming into a gap which has been otherwise declared truly unbridgeable, yet glistening. I once was a place. You have come a long way to hand me a song like that.

To think that you are a song, because a song can open and reopen the wounds of past and passing. And when you cared to roll over those immaculate burns, nothing came out healed. Now the suture does not quite appear as a mere buzz as dead blood threads keep seeping through the parchment. What is it a song, a brooding beak, or an engine blowing smoke, a falsetto of that kind?

You as a song, because a song flows down to read the retreat address over and over and fails. Flow is something that is innate to the song. And flow holds at its root an incessant movement, a reforming displacement, an eternal slippage, a bubbling friction being dragged away from where it was previously remembered. The journey of the song could only mean the drifting waves that undercut the shoreline to carry it off. Am I to think of you as a song slipping away from the root harbored deep in the throat? No oysterhood, no cries, I know the song always riles the bottom of the root.

Unclaimed

Shan Spradlin

Your words as mist.
Soft
fragrance of angel's bloom. Rapture.
Trumpeting inside my lungs. Your neck
leaves the corner pillow.
Warm
with lavender I breathe you. I
lay
tulips across your naked
shoulder.
Dipping beneath unfinished
dreams
I shape my arms around you.
Only
with fingerprints I touch your
sleepy
hair. Silk between us now.
Rain
drowns our shaded
windows.
A splenetic sky kicks lightning
down
the alley. Below I count
seconds
between booming rooftops.
Still. You are not
Disturbed.

Agony

Jagari Mukherjee

The veiled sculpture that Ali
creates of Maryam in
Dokhtar Irooni has come back
to haunt me after ten years…

Each word I write for you
is a block of marble -- each sentence
an imperfect sculpture of the infatuation
that is you...

I wish my fingers could chisel you
out of the intricate design of every rose,
from each piece of terracotta and jeweled lacquer
in both prose and verse...

(Since I cannot speak your name)

I long to
sew you into a green velvet leaf
plant you in the center of stars
compose you in a sonata
carry you in the dark like a lantern...

All the while burning, burning, burning
in the agony of the sculptor
dumb with desire

Ref: Dokhtar Irooni (Persian Girl) is an Iranian movie released in 2003.

Gleanings

Winston Derden

remnant memories elide
into stringless beads,

mutable, beautiful,
pointless understanding,

love an old injury conjoined by scars,
tears the vocabulary of comprehension

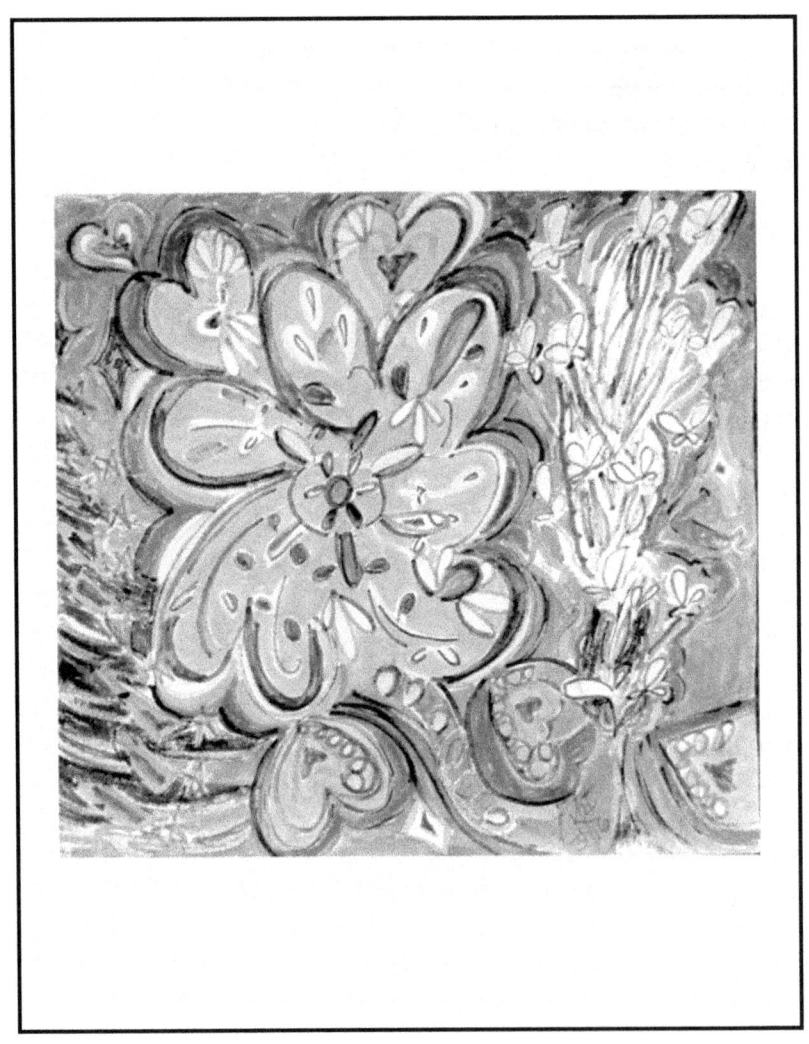

"Untitled drawing" by Kat Copeland

Elements Part 1

Srividya Sivakumar

I
Air
The air is an old-fashioned ironing box.
It's metallic black hot and whips people into shape.
Shapeless shapes of dust swirling red cheeks radiating dry throat aching slippers melting into the ground shape.
The air is searing, speaking the novena of consent and desire.
This air is a lustful beast armed to its teeth with diamonds in its navel and waist chains with keys.
It whips your clothes away so that finally you are naked and all your secrets are revealed.
Each scar, each subtraction, each stretch mark each stake in the heart.

II
Earth
The earth is your sorrow and it is greater than mine.
It is piled high and even the ants that burrow in it
are crying bitter formic tears.
No matter the defeat, your loss is greater.
I lost a tooth. You lost your voice.
Our river ran dry. Your freshwater spring has disappeared.
The roof of my house needs repairing.
Your home was devoured by termites and silverfish.
I lost my heart. You lost your cause.
We compare sorrow like it's a pissing match and you have to win.
You feed on pain like it is the cocoa that the world is running out of.
No chocolate for trite days and dry days but your sorrow will always remain.
Your martyrdom demands huge sacrifice.
My head bent at the altar, I pay top dollar for you to win this particular game.

Elements - Part 2

Srividya Sivakumar

III
Fire

The ceremonial fire in the prayer hall is my heart.
It's the eternal flame of the unknown soldier.
It is guarded at not too great a peril but with fervour that is quite unmatched.
This heart can rise up like flames tend to, neither disciplined nor bothered about lives and boundaries. It can question a tongue held in check, in cheek and make it regret it ever tried to be anything but its own self.
The heart can demand answers, hold a mirror up, burnish the metal of your soul made strong by fire.
Red but gentle, hurtful but loving, required in the cold and necessary in the summer.
The heart does not know Fahrenheit. When you're done, it disappears.

IV
Water

Water is the love that courses through my hair.
It's slick with smooth talk, laden with the perfume of promises and flowing like a river that changes its course.
                This love is my unbecoming.
It is my doom and my destiny.
                              It is my meeting the sea.
It is in the sweat of sweet lovemaking and a swig from his whisky glass.
This water moves sluggishly, hesitantly not knowing if it wants to swirl in a pool or pool at my feet.
Not knowing if it wants to bind
                to cleave to wear down stone or just move on.
      This water love is
             a conundrum that carries no easy answers.

V
Space

Space is the price I pay for wanting you in my life.

You have moved mountains and continents so many times
that I have lost your last known location.

This void   is what fills my life.

Every book, every adventure, every bit of leaf and lawn
is suffused with aether.
There is space between nail and finger.

Between touch and testament.

Between want and wanderlust.

This enormous　　　　　　chasm pulls everything to it
and leaves nothing for feasting.

It sings a siren song

but the moment I get close, it withdraws.

Someday, you say, we will all be the void.

We will all be space.

Yes, but right now, when I am starlight,

why make me ache?

Waltz

Elina Petrova

After your birthday dinner, you said life
didn't turn out the way you wanted.
Then, who wanted the way it turned out?
If no one, why did it turn out that way?
I wanted a son, summers in a fishermen's
village, and an endless book where seagulls
would dispute the catch of memories
until silence dims the coral ashes of a shore
and other planets rise – with methane rivers
that cleave their blue craggy surfaces
and geyser vapors that form into frozen particles
the size of our house, rotate on a carousel
of orbital rings, gravitational ripples.
At night I hear not only cicadas and alarms
from distant parking lots, but the silence
whose interpreting is my gift on Earth.
I enter it – a swimmer, who used to long
for a lonely blue lap, a lover who's learned
thousands of paths to almost unsharable joy,
quiet ratios of musica universalis.
With you we are music. For you I dye
my nickel hair black and fit into jeans I wore
at seventeen, when – on foggy November stops –
I waited for the lightened bus to take me uptown.
There, after a day of threading water pipes
at a factory, I would watch couples promenade
along dark boulevards, wrought banisters
run staircases as musical staves. Elegant
bookshelves and paintings behind high
windows made me think of lives that turned out
the way they wanted – clusters of grapes
to minuets by Rameau. I cupped my hands
to light a cigarette in the drizzle of an emptying
boulevard and drifted into idle reveries like those
about couples waltzing at a candlelit Viennese
Ball, and my grandparents who never danced,
but survived the famine together.
Frosted silence congealed puddles, creased
my movements when I struck a match. Planets
rotated, looking down at the insignificance
of any human story, but – in many years –

when I met you, something in their equations
changed, the music in a darkened
concert hall stopped being an oboe solo
under a solitary spotlight. Gentle melodies
wove into a bassline with a steady heartbeat,
waltzed in a warming silence the way
I wanted, the way it turned out.

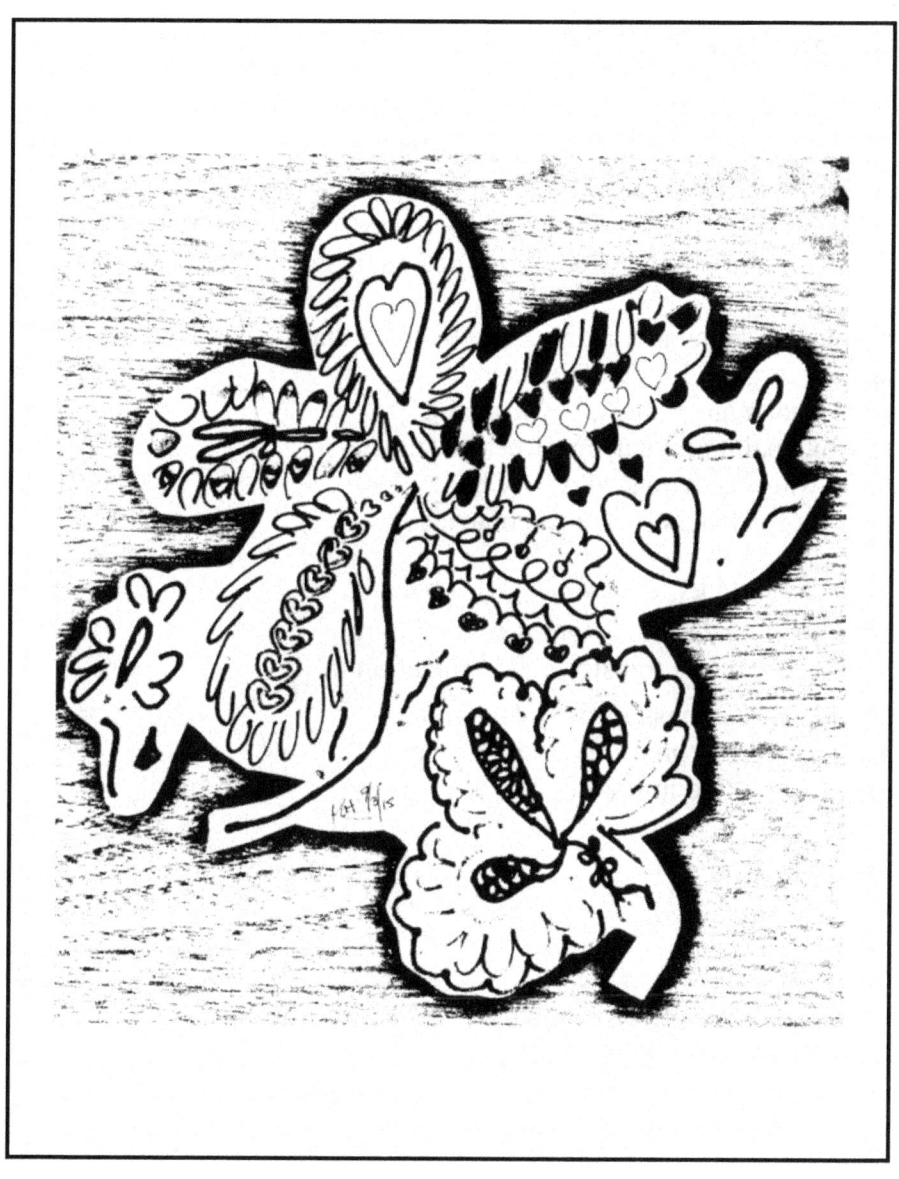

"Untitled drawing" by Kat Copeland

Protection

Elina Petrova

Selfish to say, I loved the gentleness with which you
treated the wounded half of me that you couldn't understand
yet carried like tempered glass that is but glass: do not
drop, crush, break, or shake. And now, when we catch up
on sleep in adjacent bedrooms, it's already cause to lose

and look for each other in a dream. You walk panicked
among the high-rise towers you used to work in – tilted,
enclosing the sky. I awake in Moscow in an unfriendly
rented flat where I can't find your weathered slippers
that I used to mock, but their absence makes my heart stagger.

The cars, coats dashing under a balcony raise the tachycardia
of the muted rhapsody in grey. I type a message to you
whose lengthy lines smoke and vanish. I type again:
the turquoise and white paint of a narrow street in Tunisia
leads to the museum where they placed on my head
the ancient brocade fez for loners seeking le marriage.

I type and see drizzly haze in Kiev – a mosaic of wet
maple leaves on the green and bronze domes of the Lavra
Monastery of the Caves, where I translate The Protection

of the Most-Holy Theotokos[1] mass for you, and you
look at me as usual: a foreigner missing the point, yet
catching something much more important than what I say.

---

[1] *Called Pokrova (cloak, shroud) in Ukraine, The Protecting Veil of the Theotokos is an Eastern Orthodox feast referring to the Intercession of the Holy Virgin. On the day of this feast, October 14, many Russian-speaking single women pray they will meet and marry the right man.*

Ulcus Tangere

Sanjeev Sethi

Stravaging metes and bounds we inched
to inner chambers. Bounty of feelings and
barren nowness. Excess is antagonistic to
coupledom. Emails never touch-typed,
hesitancies froze our hum. Music in breath
cached flavors close to textures. Antsy half
sentences were eager to sign fluent twists.
Some are for postmortems.

Dinner
After Yoko

Jessica Rowshandel

Listen to the heartbeat of a fork
as it sits on the plate.
Listen to the heartbeat of a fork
as you bring it to your mouth.

Take the fork and hit your glass
hard -- until the glass breaks.
Mend the broken pieces into a flat sheet.

This is a map of your heartbeat
as you eat your dinner.

Count the beats.
Say, "I love you"
in as many languages
and to twice the people.

After Twenty-Five Years

Robert Cooperman

After twenty-five years,
I run into this old friend. We hug

a long, long time, as if afraid
if we let go, we'll lose contact again.

We talk about the old times,
only to hear Zach's divorced
that two other friends have gone

where we'll all go to.
Me? My life pretty boring,

Beth and me happy to be living here again
after too many strange sojourns.

We exchange cellphone, email addresses,
talk about seeing another old friend,

about hiking in the foothills.
So good to see him again,

forgetting why we lost touch
in the first place.

In a Universe Where

Josh Dale

The joists don't creak
with every step
and the neighbors downstairs
cease their chatter to sonar
my way to bed like rats.

The audience cheers yet
doesn't sound like a
live audience when tuned
into different shows in primetime
waning Americana after the news
counts the body bags.

The young woman leaps from the car
embraces her lover with gray suitcase
A kiss locked in timeless Virginia
hands around the neck a dainty noose
a foot dangling in gravity forever
as if the war is over
and I'm just flying by.

A Kiss From the Wind

Susan Mitchell

The wind blows his kiss against my cheek.
A leaf falls from a tree and glides to the ground.
Overcast skies are a lid on the world.
I wonder where he might be.
The wind chimes on the porch
could be his laughter
or just a reminder of it.
His face, in many shapes of smiles, greets me
at home but he does not speak
though I talk to him.
He said he loved me before he
hung up the phone.
I told him I loved him too.
It is as true today as it was then.
Some days, even more.
This young man I had brought
into the world, let me see his life
from beginning to end --
something a mother
is not supposed to do.
But if she does, the love
never diminishes.
It never subsides.
The love is like an ocean:
ever present, forever deep,
always in motion, and,
able to become a hurricane.
When my ocean becomes a hurricane
I let the wind bring his kiss to my cheek,
the wind chimes remind me of his laughter.

Out of the Blue

Susan Moorhead

He was afraid of bridges. He wasn't and then suddenly, he was.
I couldn't understand it. My fears are life long, born young and
bred deep. I know them like I know my oldest friends. How
could a person just become afraid of a thing that didn't bother
him before? I would think this as we pulled to the side of the
road to switch seats so that I could do the stint over whatever
bridge needing crossing. He had always hated heights, maybe
this was just a variation on a theme. I didn't mind, what I hated

was his stoic insistence on trying to cross over anyway, when
his giving in to fear turned into anger at himself that hovered
over the rest of the road trip like a sulky cloud. He was fiercely
afraid and then, months later, the terror subsided into that dull ache
of a lifelong hindrance. He took measured breaths and drove
over bridges, fighting his own inclinations all the way. I thought
it a shame, missing out on bridges. The rising arches
like unfolding wings, the tangible symbolism of crossing over,

just the very here to thereness of them. On a Vermont vacation,
I left him and our son bank side while I explored an abandoned
train trestle, all broken, rotted boards and deliriously beautiful
rusted metal work. I went farther than I meant to go, looking
with my camera's eye rather than common sense. Suddenly
I was stuck, unsure of how to move, the gaps of board boasting
of the drop below. "Here," my husband's voice surprised me.
He stood on a metal railing just inches away. "Take my hand."
We worked our way back to certain ground where our son stood
shaking his head at two fools on a bridge going there to here.

Memory

Jessica Goody

Everything he loves about her is gone.
Her face is frozen, blank as new paper, the smooth dark
curves of brow faded to whiteness, the narrow, elegant mouth
rimmed with the pinpricks of dimples drags now,

the dimples no longer flickering in the curve of her cheek.
Her skin is slack now and creased with wrinkles, the joints stiff
and swollen. Her long fingers are gnarled and crone-cold,
her legs etched with blue veins mapping their decades together.

Every day he visits, waiting to see some spark of memory
in her eyes, the knowledge of his presence, forgotten yet familiar.
He holds her cold hands, scrubbing them between his own to warm
them, and links their fingers, stroking her knuckles with his thumb.

The Marriage

Kiriti Sengupta

I'm happily flaunting my marital status
for ages. Seeing this earnest unification
a friend probes the composite. I add to
his impressions:
It is the wife, who keeps trust on the consortium.

A Language Foreign

Melissa Chappell

I didn't know.

I didn't know,
shivering in a sheet
as you walked out the door
without a backward glance,
why you could not
tell me something,
anything,
to keep me warm
as winter neared my door.

All I had was
the empty bottle of scotch,
abandoned,
on my kitchen counter.

You will nourish
my dreams,
the memory
of you in me,
the movement
of time passing away.

And I,
wrapping myself
around you,
a wisteria vine,
holding onto you,
fighting to keep you
from slipping
out of this matrix
into someone else's
vocabulary,
becoming the subject
of someone else's
sentence.

I didn't know.

I didn't know
that when you walked
out of the door,
you walked
into the convoluted
syntax
of my mind.

You didn't know,
our silent conversation
was a language of the heart.

In the days ahead,
my mind will spin,
conjugating the verbs,
declining the nouns,
until no answer is reached,
only that I loved you,
only that to you,
it was a language foreign.

Metropolis

John Kojak

You began as a fervent light
        in the distance
Upon first glance,
        a thing bright but minute
But I can see now that
        you are no small thing
You are a colossus,
        a giant sprawling metropolis
Replete with highways,
        bi-ways, and busy streets
I like to wander through
        their splendor and decay
Hoping to find the vibrant heart,
        the main square
Where you will be waiting,
        an answer to my prayer

Where is Love?

JeanMarie Olivieri

Love keeps the stars in the sky,
I've heard the poets say.

Such lofty thoughts leave no room
for the golden rule.

Science searches the heavens for dark matter.
Look no further than the heart of man.

Where can I find the higher, bigger, planet-spinning stuff?
Here, with you.

Addressing the Hall of Poets
(an occasional poem)

James B. Nicola

You were two, nine months before you were,
As those two, long before they were, were two.
Which makes you, once upon a time, four.
Before that, eight, sixteen, and thirty-two;
Still earlier, one thousand twenty-four.
Go back yet more to see that what you were
Was what I was: every soul that was,
As everyone who is, like us, once was,
Unmet stranger, Cousin, Sister- Brother-
Poet, All-Consuming Self of You,
Miraculously Me and every other
Who has yet to be conceived of,
The End of All Begun: One

Love

Awakening

Daginne Aignend

Gingerly,
I move forwards
step by step
I'm nervous
scared that
someone
might see me
Once outside,
I find out
that I never
noticed before
how bright
the sun shines

Sitting Zazen on the Downtown 4 Train

Claudine Nash

Wherever you are in your
small corner, there is a
train rolling through you
carrying all the beings who

have ever loved the dull
colors of something or
someone to life. And

though the walls of your
room may be worn and
thick with neglect, if

you stretch this moment

so thin

that the enemy in your head
can't whisper,

you may feel the cars
of this train speed through
all the empty stations you
have ever known,

so much so

that when you glance
at the strangers who pass
through this dim and
icy morning,

the deepest tints
and hues within you
start to vibrate,

you detect

the secret sound
the world makes

when it speaks all
its languages at once.

Magnolias

Claudine Nash

Listen, I
need to say
just once in
this lifetime,
that when I
look at you
I see a
landscape,
alive and
soaked in
magnolias,
where I find
myself home
in fields I
have never
and always
known, to
which each
and every
turn, I
return.

One

Usha Akella

My pen skips too easily to write another alphabet,
of another time—quills, blue skies, the flight of birds,
woods and lakes, walking, always walking even before
we walked, so when we walk now Life is memory.
How do I know a Time before this time?
Easily, the past quietly rows itself on the lake of the
present, And your eyes still—all Time in them.

I watch myself as a gladiator watches his moves
drawn to his opponent, his altar—quietly. This one
teaches me patience. When is the lake still?
When it perfectly embraces the tree at its edge,
transposed without a tremor, one lake, one tree, one.

Sufi Poems

Usha Akella

1.

Do not recognize,
Do not find me, I plead,
Do not come,
Do not call, I beg.

Do not be the perfume in all things,
the thumbprint, the signature,
Do not brand me as yours,
Don't stand at the door of my eyes
and look out into the world,
Do not be the birth of my breath,
Do not be the screen of my mind,
The ink in my pen,
Do not be kind.

Do not be the outpost of my heart,
Do not enter,
Do not occupy this house,
Don't hold my hand,
Don't hold me close,
Don't be the present
Or the past,
Don't become my future.

Do not be the pores in this skin,
Do not be this solitude,
Do not be the space between my words,
Do not be the essence of all teachings,
Do not go into the world,
Do not come back to me,
Do not search across time,
Don't wipe my tears,
or hold my anguish quivering like a deer in a fence,
And then vanish into ether like curling incense.

Do not be the gold in my soul,
Do not be the hours of the day,
Do not be the beats in my heart,
Do not be the seasons that turn,
Do not be the dust on my soles.

Do not smile,
Do not be gentle,
Do not be the night sky under which I lie,
Don't be the promise of the stars,
Or the games of the moon,
Don't come too late, don't come too soon.

Do not be the rising sun
and its garments of heat,
Do not be the setting sun
and its garments of sleep
Do not be the incandescence of my dreams.

Do not be the simplicity of the child,
Do not be the laughter in the breeze,
And the fire that burns in me,
Do not be the embrace against the tides of life,
Do not be the sun giving me light,
Do not give names
as bridges to find you,
Do not leave your footprints as clues,
Do not brand the universe with your signs
Do not call me 'mine.'

Do not bless me
and remove your hand from my head,
Do not leave my heart vulnerable as
a new born calf,
Do not leave me living,
Do not leave me dead.

Do not be the branches
hurtling to the sky,
Do not be the trunk planted in the earth,
Do not be the surrender of the flowers,
Don't be the worm turning the soil,
Or the butterfly challenging the air,
Do not be the blessing of falling leaves,
Or the oil in which I burn,
Do not be the grass trampled under my feet,

Do not, do not be the seed in my heart,
And the river in my veins,
Do not be my pleasure or my pain,
The things I lose, the things I gain.

Do not be the road I travel,
Or the incense of the days,
Do not be the patience between meetings,
Do not be the things this poem doesn't say,
Do not be my waiting,
Do not be my obedience,
Do not teach me surrender,
Do not be the humility that rejects this poem,
Do not be the silence shielding us from the world,
Do not teach me restraint,
Do not be gentle my Master,
Do not melt me in hidden fires,
Do not pull the wires like a puppeteer.

I am breaking breaking breaking.

2.
Heaven has gone.
               Gone!
   The world is dimmed.
      The heart is cold
         with stalactites of ice.
Grey ash this world, inside and out,
an eyeball in the grave.

Behind this screen I watch moving images,
       the senseless gaiety in
          people seeming to know where they go,
where they've been, where they will end.

Like a squirrel I scamper from branch to branch
     reckless with grief, homeless,
        a circus unto myself,
      under an unconcerned sky.

Someone tell me, this heart is a planet
              and it is here that you roam.
                    Please.

3.
Which is the palace of illusions?
        this grief?
        this heart?
        this poem?
        your silence?

4.
There's a chair here   plastic of some kind,
                nothing fancy.

Only, that it held a form, two weeks ago
        as a spoon holds honey,

                      and now it could be a
                      swan,
                                    a white lotus,
        my journey's end,
      the shape of my waiting,
            the palm of my devotion,
                an emblem of silence,
                    a teaching, like the flower of Buddha,
                    holy feet.

        I sit in it at times,
              your unequal   but unashamed,

            And I am held   by what holds you.

Post Script: Love is You

Love is being capitalized for the entirety of this piece of 'deliberate prose', because I am referring to it as a physical being, almost in the sense of a goddess, but a tad lower on the spectrum where humanity lies. I often ask my friends, acquaintances, colleagues, and family what their personal definition of what Love is. I am always fascinated by each individual answer. When they return the question, I hypocritically tell them that I believe it has no definition. It is what I have concluded over the years. It is often debatable that Love is the most powerful emotion, but in my lowly opinion, I believe it is the most beautiful and the most mystical emotion…and it cannot be tainted. When people tamper with it, the face of Love often backfires on them. Unfortunately, I have been both an observer and a participant in this matter. I will not dive bomb into the doldrums of the past, for that is what a fraction of my confessional poetry is for.

Time and time again, science has disproved many aspects of Love, including the very concept of Love itself. However, it does not take away from the series of experiences one endures over time. Love takes on many forms and one never senses its presence. It may greet you as an ally during certain occasions, while on others, it may appear as an arch nemesis, testing the level of your vulnerability and weak points. Love is an ambiguous sort of character, an apparition that is easy on the eyes, a beckoning voice that leads you to absolutely nowhere. How I am thankful for the somewhat omnipresent role it randomly plays. As children, we are told numerous legends about Love. We are told of its triumphs and tragedies, its trepidations and its trials, and its many facets and attitudes. It is up to us whether or not we choose to carry the torch with the flames of Love attached to it.

In this anthology, Love is explored beyond the lines of Infinity. We delve into Love and loss, forbidden Love, first Love and infatuation, the differences between Love and lust, and much more. Briefly mentioning confessional poetry, I often spot a pattern when reading Love poetry anthologies. There are many instances where the author places themselves in their work and the words are enhanced. For this particular theme, that method works wonders. This can be spotted in pieces such as 'Five Things I Should Tell You' by Lennart Lundh, 'This Evening is Not Meant for Love Poems' by Debasish Parashar, and many others. I have also noticed that pieces that are very few lines can speak volumes. This is common in the field of poetry in general, but all it takes to make a mental earthquake happen is one meaning, relatable or not. People often cling to what means to them the most, which is quite reasonable. In this case, I think of the following piece:

Untitled

Margarita Serafimova

I was in love,
and the body was everything,
and the body did not matter.

Just those lines alone sent me into a maelstrom where there was no recovery. As usual, it is left up to the reader to decide what the meaning is. For some, it may be fairly obvious. For others, they prefer to dig deeper than the average literary interpreter does.

At this point in my life, I would say that Love and I might have waged war against one another in the past, but we have come to a reasonable truce...for the time being. We do not speak often, for Love has taught me how to do so myself. I must extend another lowly opinion in saying that Love for the self, next to Love for family and friends, reigns supreme over any kind of Love, even in the romantic sense. It has sent me into multiple metamorphoses (including switching from hopeless romantic to closet romantic) and each time I exit the cocoon, I learn a bit more about myself in that sense. I am still learning to Love myself through improving my mental and physical state, but I feel like I have stepped forward more than I have in the past few years. I still continue to write and occasionally sing about it, as it is my guilty pleasure among my eclectic topics.

Through humor, meditation in any form, and creation, anything is possible. True Love does exist, for I have witnessed it countless times. However, it is not essential in this life. It is but a garnish or a seasoning on top of a banquet. As my father has stated, "There are gems in the human rock pile." If that gem finds you, Dear Reader, hold on for dear life. You will not regret this journey. I promise you that and much more, but I prefer that you find out for yourself. Poetry lives. Long live the arts.

E.M. Wise

Acknowledgements

The following is a list of previously published poems in the order that they appear in the anthology:

Susan Moorhead- A Love Poem: *Notes for the Journey*, Origami Poems Project
Susan Moorhead – Cicada Moon: *River, River*
Debasish Parashar - This Evening is Not for Love Poems: *Praxis Magazine*
Debasish Parashar – Love in Less: *Enclave-Entropy*
Zack Rogow- The Only Boy in Ballet Class: *My Mother and the Ceiling Dancers*, Kattywompus Press
Zack Rogow – Symmetron: You and Brother Will: *The Number Before Infinity,* Scarlet Tanager Books
Lisa Rhodes-Ryabchich – We are Beautiful Like Snowflakes, *We are Beautiful Like Snowflakes,* Finishing Line Press
Len Lundh – Five Things I Should Tell You: *Poems Against Cancer*
Debasis Mukhopadhyay- Song & the Bottom of the Root: *The Curly Mind*
Susan Moorhead – Out of the Blue: *Woman Around Town*
Daginne Aignend – Awakenings: *Inventives*
Claudine Nash – Sitting Zazen on the Downtown 4 Train: *Breadcrumbs Magazine*
Claudine Nash – Magnolias: *Yellow Chair Review*

About the Authors

Sheikha A. is from Pakistan and United Arab Emirates. Her work has been published and anthologized widely in numerous venues by different presses. A record of all her publications can be found at sheikha82.wordpress.com.

Daginne Aignend is a pseudonym for the Dutch writer, poetess, photographic artist Inge Wesdijk. She liked hard rock music, fantasy books, and loved her animals. Daginne had been published in many poetry journals, magazines and anthologies. She sadly lost her battle with cancer before the publication of this book.

Usha Akella has authored four books of poetry. She read with a group of eminent South Asian Diaspora poets at the House of Lords in June 2016. She was selected as a Cultural Ambassador for the City of Austin for 2015. She is the organizer of 'Matwaala' the first South Asian Diaspora Poets Festival in the US. She has won literary prizes (Nazim Hikmet award, Open Road Review Prize and Egan Memorial Prize)She is the organizer of 'Matwaala' the first South Asian Diaspora Poets Festival in the US. She has won literary prizes (Nazim Hikmet award, Open Road Review Prize and Egan Memorial Prize). She hold an MA in Creative Writing from Cambridge University, UK.

Born in north Minnesota, **Margaret Anderegg** was the seventh of ten children on their family farm. She earned AA degree in Elementary Education, married, moved to Texas and raised five children. Her sister-in-law Mary, a lifelong diabetic with a kidney transplant, could not bear children. Adopting Lucas (Korea) exalted her life, and his.

A four-time Pushcart Prize, five-time Best of the Net & Bettering American Poetry nominee, **Lana Bella** is an author of three chapbooks, *Under My Dark* (Crisis Chronicles Press, 2016), *Adagio* (Finishing Line Press, 2016), and *Dear Suki: Letters* (Platypus 2412 Mini Chapbook Series, 2016).

Don Beukes is a writer of poetry and short fiction and Pushcart Nominee. Originally from South Africa, he is also a reviewer and translates poetry into Afrikaans. His books include *The Salamander Chronicles* (CTU), *Icarus Rising-Volume 1* (ABP) and *In Pursuit of Poetic Perfection* (Libbo Publishers and Milborrow Media, South Africa).

Annie Bien has written two poetry books—*Under Shadows of Stars* (Kelsay Books, 2017) and *Plateau Migration* (Alabaster Leaves Press, 2012). The Soho Theatre Company in London awarded her with her first seed commission. She translates Tibetan Buddhist scriptures into English through 84000: Translating the Words of the Buddha. http://anniebien.com

R. Bremner of Glen Ridge via Lyndhurst, NJ, USA, writes of incense, peppermints, and the color of time. His latest books are *Hungry Words* (Alien Buddha Press), *Chambers of a Heart* (New Feral Press), *Absurd* (Cajun Mutt Press), and *Ektomorphic* (Presa Press). Ron has thrice won Honorable Mention in the Allen Ginsberg awards, and invites you to visit his Instagram poetry at beat_poet1 and Absurdist_poet.

Matthew Borczon is a writer from Erie, Pa. he has published nine books so far. The most recent being In the years since the War through Cajun Mutt Press. Matthew has been nominated for both a pushcart and best of the Net and was the recipient of an emerging artists grant from the Erie Arts and culture organization. He publishes widely in the small press and is married for 22 years to a woman he does not deserve. They have 4 wonderful children who give him all the joy in the world

Adam Levon Brown is an internationally published poet and author in 14 countries. He has had his work translated in Spanish, Albanian, Arabic, and Afrikaans. Boasting over 300 published pieces, you can find his writing at such publications as *Burningword Literary Journal, Zany Zygote Review, Epigraph,* and *Angel City Review.*

Making her life in rural South Carolina, much of **Melissa Chappell's** inspiration comes from living on land that has been in her family for six generations. She loves its woodlands and open spaces and diversity of life, which find their way into much of her poetry.

Robert Cooperman's latest full-length collection is *Their Wars* (Kelsay Books). Liquid Light Press recently brought out the chapbook, *Saved By The Dead.* Forthcoming from Lithic Press is *The Devil Who Raised Me* and from Main Street Rag, *That Summer.* Cooperman lives in Denver with the love of his life, his wife Beth.

Josh Dale is a bicyclist, beer enthusiast, Bengal cat dad, open mic goer, and an MA candidate at Saint Joseph's University. His work and press have appeared in *Breadcrumbs Mag, Huffington Post, Page & Spine, vox poetica,* and others. He's the founder and editor-in-chief of Thirty West Publishing House.

Mikayla Davis is a recent graduate of the MFA program at the University of Central Arkansas. She's a poet who probably spends too much time gaming, but has somehow still managed to get works published in *Blue Heron Review, Ghost City Press, Gold Dust Magazine*, and others.

Winston Derden is a poet and fiction writer residing in Houston, Texas. His poetry publications include *New Texas, Blue Collar Review, Harbinger Asylum, Big River Poetry Review, Illya's Honey, Barbaric Yawp, 'Merica Magazine, Soft Cartel, Down in the Dirt, Plum Tree Tavern,* and several anthologies.

Mary Elmahdy is headstrong and stubborn, a folk music lover, a romantic without romance. She travels the world, discovers life, gives what she can, and leaves with no regrets. She listens to what others say and then follows her heart. Currently, she lives and writes in Tucson, AZ.

Michael Estabrook has been publishing his poetry in the small press since the 1980s. Hopefully with each passing decade the poems have become more clear and concise, succinct and precise, more appealing and "universal." He has published over 20 collections, a recent one being *Bouncy House*, edited by Larry Fagin (Green Zone Editions, 2014).

Red Focks is an American author, publisher, and folk artist. In addition to his operating Alien Buddha Press, Red has been featured by 17 Numa, Nixes Mate, Madness Muse Press; and his novel *Haight* was published in 2018 by Cajun Mutt Press. Red is the head writer of the graphic Novel *American Antihero*. His other books include *Duffy Street & Other Dubious Incidents, The Philanthropist's Suicide,* and *36 Haikus and a Horror Story.*

Kamilah Glover is a thriving author, healer and mother. Kamilah has a passion for the uplifting and upkeep of women, mothers and young ladies. She has been developing her writing career with two self published books and numerous local newspaper publications. Kamilah loves to spend time caring for her son and daughter, who are her inspiration. She hopes to be a light for other single mothers struggling find their voice today's complicated culture.

Ethan Goffman's poems have appeared in *BlazeVox, Mad Swirl, Madness Muse,* and *Setu*. As a journalist, he has extensive publications on environmental and transit issues. He currently writes for Mobility Lab and teaches at Montgomery College.

Robert Milton Ingram writes poetry, songs, and gay fiction that explore themes of diversity, social justice, self-discovery, and human potential. His poems have been published in several journals and anthologies. Some of his work can also be found on his Facebook fan page as well as www.youtube.com/user/IngramMusic.

Stephanie L. Harper is author of the chapbooks, *This Being Done* (Finishing Line Press) and *The Death's-Head's Testament* (Main Street Rag). Her poems appear in such journals as *Slippery Elm, Isacoustic*, Rat's Ass Review, Panoply, Underfoot Poetry,* and elsewhere. She lives with her family in Hillsboro, OR.

John Kojak's short stories have been published in *Beyond Imagination, Down In The Dirt, Third Wednesday, Bête Noire,* and *Pulp Modern* magazines. His poetry has appeared in *Poetry Quarterly, Dual Coast, The Stray Branch, The Literary Commune, Dime Show Review, The Los Angeles Review of Los Angeles, Chronogram,* and *Harbinger Asylum*.

Luke Kuzmish is a poet and recovering addict. He hails from Erie, Pennsylvania. When not shoveling snow or eating mercury-riddled fish, Luke has written three chapbooks: Quetiapine Dreams, twentysomething (Poets' Hall Press, 2014), and Little Hollywood (Alien Buddha Press, 2018).

Kristin LaFollette is a PhD candidate at Bowling Green State University and is a writer, artist, and photographer. She is the author of the chapbook, *Body Parts* (GFT Press, 2018). You can visit her on Twitter at @k_lafollette03 or on her website at kristinlafollette.com

Lennart Lundh is a poet, short-fictionist, historian, and photographer. His work has appeared internationally since 1965.

Joan McNerney's poetry has been included in numerous literary magazines such as *Seven Circle Press, Dinner with the Muse, Moonlight Dreamers of Yellow Haze, Blueline,* and *Halcyon Days*. Three Bright Hills Press Anthologies, several *Poppy Road Review Journals*, and numerous *Kind of A Hurricane Press* publications have accepted her work. Her latest title is *Having Lunch with the Sky* and she has four Best of the Net nominations.

Susan J. Mitchell has been anthologized in *Motif: Writing by Ear* (Motif Books, 2009) and *Motif: Come What May* (Motif Books, 2010). Two of Susan's books include the award winning *Snapshots* (Heart to Heart Publishing, 2013), and *After the Heroin: A Mother's Story in Poetry* (Old Seventy Creek Publishing, 2017).

Susan Moorhead's poetry has ridden on buses in Connecticut to celebrate National Poetry Month, become paper fish and magic leaves while teaching children, and guided adults to share their life stories in poems. Her poetry, stories, and essays have appeared in numerous print and online journals and anthologies and have been nominated three times for a Pushcart prize. Her chapbook, *The Night Ghost*, was published with Finishing Line Press.

Leah Mueller is the author of two chapbooks and four books. Her latest book, *Bastard of a Poet* was published by Alien Buddha Press in June 2018. Leah's work appears in *Blunderbuss, The Spectacle, Outlook Springs, Drunk Monkeys, Atticus Review, Your Impossible Voice*, and other publications.

Jagari Mukherjee is a poet from Kolkata, India. Her first collection of poems entitled *Blue Rose* was published in May 2017 by Bhashalipi. She is a Best of the Net 2018 nominee, a Bear River 2018 alumna, and the winner of the Rabindranath Tagore Literary Prize 2018 for book review.

Debasis Mukhopadhyay is the author of the chapbook *kyrie eleison or all robins taken out of context* (Finishing Line Press, 2017). His poems have appeared in *Erbacce, Posit, Words Dance, I am not a silent poet, Better than Starbucks*, & elsewhere. Debasis lives & writes in Montreal, Canada. Blog: https://debasismukhopadhyay.wordpress.com/

James B. Nicola's poems have appeared frequently in *Harbinger Asylum*. His nonfiction book *Playing the Audience* won a *Choice* award. His poetry collections are *Manhattan Plaza* (2014), *Stage to Page: Poems from the Theater* (2016), *Wind in the Cave* (2017), and *Out of Nothing: Poems of Art and Artists* (2018). Anton Yakovlev was one of the poets in the Hall of Poets that inspired the present poem.

The author of five chapbook collections, three micro-chapbooks and a mini-digital chapbook, **Robert Okaji** lives in the Texas hill country, where he occasionally works on a ranch. His work has also appeared in such publications as *MockingHeart Review, Crannóg, Reservoir, Vox Populi, Eclectica, Boston Review, Panoply, Oxidant|Engine* and elsewhere.

JeanMarie Olivieri is freelance writer, poet and aspiring comic who believes poetry can change the world. She lives in North Carolina where there are so many writers you can't throw a rock without hitting one. But don't throw rocks! Follow her at https://jeanmarieolivieri.wordpress.com/.

Iris Orpi is a Filipina poet, novelist, and screenwriter living in Chicago. She is the author of the novel *The Espresso Effect* and four books of compiled poetry, including *Rampant and Golden*. She was a 2018 Pushcart Prize nominee and a 2014 Honorable Mention for the Contemporary American Poetry Prize.

Weasel Patterson is a degenerate author and The Dude of Weasel Press. In 2018, he released a chapbook of poetry titled *We Don't Make It Out Alive*. You can find him on twitter: www.twitter.com/systmaticweasel.

Debasish Parashar is a Creative Entrepreneur, Multilingual Poet and Singer/Composer based in New Delhi. He is an Assistant Professor of English Literature at Delhi University. His works have appeared in *Kweli, Sentinel Literary Quarterly, Contemporary Literary Review India, Expound, Enclave/Entropy, Five2One, Asian Signature, Praxis Magazine, SETU, World Poetry Almanac 2017-18* and elsewhere. His selected works have been translated to Serbian, Russian, Slovakian, Spanish, Indonesian, Afrikaans, Albanian, Persian among a few other languages.

Until 2007, **Elina Petrova** lived in Ukraine and worked in engineering management. She has two poetry books and many publication credits in Russian and English. Her poems have appeared in *Texas*

Review, Texas Poetry Calendars, "Poetry of the American Southwest" series and numerous anthologies. She was three times nominated for Pushcart Prize, participated as a juried poet in several poetry festivals and received Top Honors in the 2018 Ekphrastic Poetry Contest at the Friendswood Library.

Winston Plowes shares his floating home in Calderdale UK with his 16-year-old cat, Sausage. He teaches creative writing in schools and to local groups while she dreams of Mouseland. His latest collection *Tales from the Tachograph* was published jointly with Gaia Holmes in 2018 by Calder Valley Poetry. www.winstonplowes.co.uk

Lisa Rhode-Ryabchich is a University of the People professor and the author of *Opening the Black Ovule Gate*, 2018 and *We Are Beautiful like Snowflakes*, 2016, from (http://www.finishinglinepress.com). She obtained a MFA from Sarah Lawrence College and a Martha's Vineyard Institute of Creative Writing Fellowship in 2016. She is also a reader for Empire Great Jones Press. Her blog is lisarhodesryabchichpoetryblog.wordpress.com

Zack Rogow is the author, editor, or translator of twenty books or plays. His play *Colette Uncensored* had its first staged reading at the Kennedy Center in and ran in London and San Francisco. He serves as a contributor editor for *Catamaran Literary Reader*. www.zackrogow.com

Jessica Rowshandel is a freelance writer and author of the book *Lupus: 365 Tips for Living Well*. She is also an ex-social worker turned techie, back in school studying planetary geology, and started writing poetry way before any of this. To read some of her long-form work, visit jessicarowshandel dot com.

Kiriti Sengupta is an award-winning poet, translator, publisher and editor-in-chief of *Ethos Literary Journal*. He is based at Calcutta, India. More at kiritisengupta.com

Margarita Serafimova was shortlisted for Montreal Poetry Prize 2017, Summer Literary Seminars 2018, Hammond House Literary Prizes 2018; long-listed for Erbacce Poetry Prize 2018, Red Wheelbarrow 2018 Prize. She has three collections in Bulgarian, and appears in Agenda Poetry, London Grip, Trafika Europe, The Journal, A-Minor, Waxwing, Orbis, Nixes Mate, StepAway, HeadStuff, more.

Sanjeev Sethi is the author of three books of poetry. He is published in more than 25 countries. Recent credits: *Talking Writing, Poydras Review, Litbreak, Red Savina Review, The Piker Press, Poetry Super Highway, The Five-Two, Amethyst Review, Ethos Literary Journal,* and elsewhere. He lives in Mumbai, India.

Dr. Srividya Sivakumar is a poet, teacher, columnist, speaker, and a nominee for the Best of the Net anthology. She has two collections of poetry to her credit- *The Blue Note* (Writers Workshop, Kolkata, 2012) and the critically-acclaimed *The Heart is an Attic*, (Hawakal Publishers, Kolkata, 2018).

Stacey Michelle Spencer lives in Birmingham, Alabama. Her poetry has appeared recently in Birmingham Arts Journal. She also writes prose and is an artist and enthusiastic home cook. You can find her on Instagram at staceyspencer75.

S. Liam Spradlin began writing poetry on a serious note in recent months. His love for poetry has led to many of his works appearing in several journals and he looks forward to releasing his first book of poetry soon. He lives in PA with his wife and author, Kim D. Bailey.

Marianne Szlyk is a professor of English and Reading at Montgomery College. She also edits The Song Is... Her first chapbook is available online at Kind of a Hurricane Press. Her second chapbook, *I Dream of Empathy*, is available on Amazon. Her poems have appeared in *Loch Raven Review, of/with, bird's thumb, Cactifur, Mad Swirl, Solidago, Red Bird Chapbook's Weekly Read, Mermaid Mirror*, and *Resurrection of a Sunflower*, an anthology of work responding to Vincent Van Gogh's art. Some have received nominations for Best of the Net and the Pushcart Prize. Her full-length book, *On the Other Side of the Window*, is now available from Pski's Porch. http://thesongis.blogspot.com

Chuck Taylor loves living in the Texas hill country. He loves his three children, his grandchildren, and all the good women who have been a part of his life. He loves writing books and hanging out in coffee shops.

Lynn White lives in north Wales. Her work is influenced by issues of social justice and events, places and people she has known or imagined. She is especially interested in exploring the boundaries of dream, fantasy and reality. Find Lynn at: https://lynnwhitepoetry.blogspot.com and https://www.facebook.com/Lynn-White-Poetry-1603675983213077/

Myra Ward Barra is a painter and award winning poet. She serves on the boards of Alabama State Poetry Society and Writer's Anonymous. She lives on Lake Logan Martin in Pell City, Alabama with her husband, Joseph, and their cats, Solomon and Sammy.

Rania M. M. Watts dabbles in myriad of art mediums, however, is most at home with a pen, crayon, eyeliner, quill and any type of parchment. Always deemed a freak of nature because of her outlooks and perceptions, Rania's allowed her imagination to dominate her core since the age of 13 when she told Mr. N, her Grade 8 teacher, that she desperately wanted to flee to Europe with a typewriter and create poetry in fields of long grass...

Anton Yakovlev's latest chapbook is *Chronos Dines Alone*, winner of the James Tate Poetry Prize (SurVision Books, 2018). He is the author of *Ordinary Impalers* (Kelsay Books, 2017) and two prior chapbooks. His poems have appeared in *The New Yorker, The Hopkins Review, Measure, The Stockholm Review of Literature*, and elsewhere.

Chani Zwibel is the author of *Cave Dreams to Star Portals,* published by Alien Buddha Press. She is an associate editor with Madness Muse Press. She is a graduate of Agnes Scott College, who was born and raised in Pittsburgh, Pennsylvania, but now dwells in Marietta, Georgia, with her husband and their dog. She enjoys writing poetry after nature walks and daydreaming.

Z.M. Wise is a proud Illinois native from Chicago, poet, essayist, co-editor and poetry activist, writing since his first steps as a child. He is co-owner and co-editor of Transcendent Zero Press, an independent publishing house for poetry that produces an international quarterly journal known as

Harbinger Asylum. He has published four full length books of poetry, including: 'Take Me Back, Kingswood Clock!' (MavLit Press), 'The Wandering Poet' (Transcendent Zero Press), 'Wolf: An Epic & Other Poems' (Weasel Press), and 'Cuentos de Amor' (Red Ferret Press). Other than these four books, his poems have been published in various journals, magazines, and anthologies. Besides poetry and other forms of writing, his other passions/interests include professional voice acting, singing/lyricism/songwriting, playing a few instruments, fitness, and reading.

About the Editor

Claudine Nash is a psychologist and award-winning poet whose collections include *The Wild Essential* (Kelsay Books, 2017) and *Parts per Trillion (*Aldrich Press, 2016) as well as the chapbook The *Problem with Loving Ghosts* (Finishing Line Press, 2014). She also co-edited two collections for Madness Muse Press: *Destigmatized* (2017) and *In So Many Words* (2016). Her poetry has earned numerous literary distinctions including Pushcart Prize nominations and prizes from such publications and artistic organizations as Artists Embassy International, Thirty West Publishing House, The Song Is… and Eye on Life Magazine among others. Internationally published, her poems have appeared in a wide range of magazines and anthologies including *Asimov's Science Fiction*, *BlazeVOX*, *Cloudbank*, *Haight Ashbury Literary Journal* and *Dime Show Review*.

www.ingramcontent.com/pod-product-compliance
Lightning Source LLC
Chambersburg PA
CBHW081015040426
42444CB00014B/3213